Salvation

A Templars' Quest for Redemption

By

Mark A Mihalko

Books by Mark A. Mihalko

Fiction
After the Static

Poetry
Walking Before Dawn

Nonfiction
Searching the Abyss

Cover Artwork by Dejan Lazarevic.
Cover Design and Layout by Brenda Mihalko
First Ringmaster's Realm Edition, May 2017
Published in the United States of America
ISBN:1548356727
ISBN-13:9781548356729

FORWARD

It is amazing how fast time flies by. As I look at the calendar, I can't believe March has come and gone so fast. This has already been an incredible year, and I have already finished many of the challenges I set for myself at the beginning of the year.

In January, I started the final push on my first fiction novel, After the Static. Eventually, I would finish that at the beginning of March. Once I completed that, I moved on to a complete edit/rewrite of my first dark poetry book, Walking Before Dawn, which was released at the end of March. And now, I have completed another national Poetry Writing Month (NaPoWriMo), this time with something much different.

Before April rolled around and that challenge came to life, I debated with myself about how I wanted to attack the month. Inside, I knew I wanted to challenge the status quo and do something that would both be enjoyable yet difficult to achieve. I wanted to accomplish something that would push me out of my comfort zone, which is when I decided that I would take on an Epic Poem and journey into darkness.

Personally, I love the classic epics that have in many ways helped shape me as both a person and a writer. With that in mind, I wanted to try my hand at such a challenge. While this may ne reach the iconic status of Paradise Lost or Inferno, it was an endeavor that I will never forget. Inside these pages, you will find a journey toward salvation as experienced by a devout member of the Knights Templar, who was sent on a quest to ancient Levant in search of Baal, Moloch, and the Scepter of Golden Light in an attempt to redeem his order in the eyes of a splintered and corrupt church.

In some ways, this piece adds a layer to the history researched by the survivors brought to life in After the Static. Especially Malachi Isaacs, the tormented narrator, who discovered this tale while doing some more research into Moloch and the Man of the Cloth. Malachi was not present during the writing of this epic, but he did come by long enough to write our introduction.

In closing, like many out there, I am convinced that the End Times have begun and the world as we know it nears its finale. And, much like the Knights Templar, we could all use a path to salvation.

— Mark A. Mihalko

"Balance every thought with its opposition.
Because the marriage of them is the destruction of illusion."

\- Aleister Crowley

TABLE OF CONTENTS

INTRODUCTION

Hello again, I can believe that I am back at my computer. I really thought that when I finished transcribing the accounts for After the Static that I would stay away from writing. Yes, yes, I do have the blog up and running and am still diving into the legend of the Man of the Cloth, as well as working on more translations and research on the mysterious dead ends that ran into working on the book, but I never dreamt that I would be working on another manuscript.

That all changed when the voices came back after I discovered an antique scrapbook at an estate sale that seems to fall in line with our religious leader and the strange Revelation of Moloch that sat at the heart of his pilgrimage. I found it odd that I stumbled upon this work inside a locked donation box that I purchased. In many ways, it felt as if the box was calling me, and I had to buy it.

The box is marked Saint Mark the Evangelist Monastery, Summit View; an abbey that does not exist anywhere inside this small town today. Strangely, from my research, there is no specific record of this place ever existing in Summit View and those records go back to the late 1800s. However, there are tales of a monastery that once stood about five miles outside of town on the National Pike. Unfortunately, details about the location and of what transpired there are few and far between. I will keep you updated on what I find on the blog (survivingstatic.blogspot.com).

This tale is extremely interesting and seems to date back quite a few years and is written in a style that appears to be closer to a work of epic prose. Personally, I love that style, but it can be difficult to follow at times. Especially in this case, as the manuscript was handwritten and some of the pages were tattered, water damaged, and weathered. Plus, there were some strange burn marks on some of the pages, almost like someone was trying to destroy it.

All I know is that ever since I opened the case, the voices and vision have returned and I have been consumed by documenting this so the world could see it. I know, I know, this all sounds crazy. Hell, I am not sure what it means or if there is a connection to the religious leader or possibly the Man of the Cloth, I have a feeling that there is something in this account that is real and that it is somehow important to the secret hidden in this area.

Plus, as you people know if you have read After the Static or the blog, you know that I don't believe in coincidence. Which, would mean that I found this scrapbook for a reason. I may not know what that reason is, but I know it is real. With that being said, sit back for a couple hours and give this tale some of your time, I hope that you find it as enlightening as I have.

- Malachi

ACKNOWLEDGMENTS

I would like to thank all of the poets of the world, who for a month every year come together and focus on creating inspiring verse and recognizing the influence classic poetry has had on society. While this may not be the greatest epic poem ever, you have all helped me find the dedication and motivation to complete it.

CANTO 1

Into the Chasm

I

My Quest, Your Salvation

Behold the day when the exiled one rose from the East, and pestilence shuttered;
ancient evils for one scepter, a cathedral defiled, and redemption stood as
humanities final gasp. For in this man, the forsaken had hope.
(The Epistle of Anacletus to the Priory 1.7)

Father, why did Clement forsake us?
Did he not see our piety? Our deeds?

Such a dark day for humanity,
The leaders, crusaders-defiled by hypocrisy,
Falling prey to a vicious cycle of unjust torment by a false prophet;
Your devout sons, persecuted in your name,
Their humanity impaled on a fiery altar.
Their names exiled like Adam from your garden.
How dare he place us in league with Baalberith?
We stand, holy, righteous, trapped inside the turmoil of sin,
Your words, your gospel are our guiding lights within the abyss.
Now, banished to the depths of Levant, my epic quest our only hope of resurrection,
The fallen star is near, I can feel it,
The mouth of the beast, our passage to anguish, and our redemption at hand,
Asherah, no, the elder, Cain, will know the truth,
My actions and sacrifices will again justify our existence,
And upon the sated ground in Moloch's Sanctum, my destiny will be fulfilled.
The primordial demonic evils will at last perish, and my soul, our order, redeemed.

Father, will Clement forgive us?
Will he not see our piety? Our deeds?

II

Jacques' Call

The almighty spoke and the cathedral trembled; thou shall drive the infected from
Levant and into the inferno. Their sins cleansed before the left hand of the father.
The repugnant king opened his mouth at the base of the mount,
and laughed at their despair.
(The Epistle of Anacletus to the Priory 1.12)

In the dark depths, mysterious decay shrouds the eternal light,
Where the golden sands decimate all powers of might,
Where the pallid hands of life tastes the Nephilim blood,
And the seeds of evermore rise from the depths of the foreseen flood,
Bones wane and bodies entwine, hearts race-souls whine,
And within the chasm, feed the flames of lust, or lovers divine,
This excursion is just; my tortuous blades embrace illicit lips,
My shaking hands, the leather strap, impaled inside luscious hips,
Destinies fulfilled, consummated by words; unbroken bounds,
The branches stand with the heretics, no one left to be found,
Golden dawn, ancient texts, undefiled gospels, or curse,
My dreams stolen by time, love, and loss; oh God, or something much worse,
From the pit, I can hear Jacques' call,
His verse radiates among the ruins, to my knees I fall,
The golden owl upon the scepter of light,
The sacred vault trembles, please, save us from our plight,
Sadness descends upon starry nights when the loneliness calls to me -
Come to me Father, my faith wavers, please, save me.

III

Lilith's Spark

From bowels of the cathedral, the stench of evil grew and the sun wept;
inside the darkness an innocent suffers, raise your cross and sharpen thy blade,
his wisdom will guide you through salvation.
(The Epistle of Anacletus to the Priory 2.9)

Bound in white, a phantom ruse
For the meek, and the shamed sin--
Thorns of bondage aligned to amuse
Abandoned prayers, the pure must win.

Empty scriptures line the throne of gold,
Prophesy forgotten, forbidden, undone,
The deceiver spoke, her message foretold,
Praise thee, for I am the son!

Nephilim bloodlines, sacred shores
Signs of life, signs of love reborn
Death surrounds us, within vessels so pure
A tear falls into the void, my lonely heart torn.

Sheep graze, and eyeless speak,
Know naught the true meaning of revelation,
Seals broken, impale the meek,
Drink from the sanguine chalice, at last grasp for salvation.

Observe a pale horse, ordained by the tainted light,
Behold the garden, the trumpets, the wine,
Prophecies fulfilled, devastation in sight,
The mark stands ready, 264 vanish, the words divine.

Senses open, blood saturates the tide,
Putrid worms replace the despair,
The liar, the deceiver, and the blind churn the divide,
Processions of candles, tainted souls, devout beware!

The mindless and brainwashed claim to pray
And their endless verse cascades,
Words held high, calls to obey
Within the shrine and upon the altar, truths evade,

Through the door, a gentle sway
A minion or more, rising from the shade,
On faded hymns, over lovers prey,
Inside tortured foundations, whose tenants fade?

Heed thy warnings; embrace the light
Cain has fallen, the demons' lark
For beneath the Cathedral, in a tomb of might
Quatrains bleed; wounds from Lilith's Spark.

Doorways open, humanity cries
Death beyond boundaries, tainted verse etched in stone.
Virtuous believers embrace falling skies,
Demons moan, serpents rise- the righteous stand, alone.

IV

The Mounds of Desolation

Do not fear, for your pious deeds are many and I have watched your deeds, and sanctified
your path. Tolerate not the wicked men, vile creatures, and false prophets;
Go forth to rebuke them, bless them, and absolve them-
for their will has been tainted by the darkness of the golden owl.
(The Epistle of Anacletus to the Priory 2.11)

Father, how much longer am I to be trapped in this Hell?
How much longer must I bear this weight of sin?

The golden sands of Gezer fade into oblivion,
The murky depths surround me, but I have been here before,
This sea of life poisoned by the ordained,
Virtuous beliefs, destroyed by Satan's sway,
Faith crumbles, under the burden of Belial and Abaddon,
Darkness and despair abound,
Naamah rises in front of the mass,
Her followers prostrate to the false idol,
Mocking the godliness that once ruled Levant,
Defiling ageless texts, sacred scripture,
I can feel it, in Zepath, the *Daemonum Codex* inhales the blessed souls,
The angelic rhymes stir the banks,
Earthquakes touch the mountains; shake the bazaar,
Voices join the chorus of thunder, and the lighting dances,
At last, my foretold path to deliverance is in sight.

Father, is this where I will face Baal, retrieve the scepter?
Will the weight of sin finally be lifted, our order restored?

V

Zepath Shudders

The fallen king shall be reborn in flames, his depravity as legendary as your suffering.
From the depths, torment will rise and the sated scars of slaughter will appear. Be faithful,
even death cannot defeat the devout, and from the ashes, a lone tree and an angel rise.
(The Epistle of Anacletus to the Priory 2.13)

In the chambers of agony, lost within the boundaries of despair,
Where the revolting spawn of Naamah poison the air,
And the river of blood cascades through dominion,
The horde stands upon the altar, my sacred blood-their demonic communion,
Mortality lost, my mace ablaze with deliverance,
Taste the flesh, for through my fathers' blessed foundation,
And within his everlasting light, redemption can be found,
Bodies fall, Zepathr shudders, souls freed, the disemboweled corpses bound,
The scripture is just, this prophecy true,
The infections inside Marduks' lair awaits, his impaled offering in view,
Where is Reric? His mortal pleas echoed across this forsaken plain,
His anguished call soaked in blood; his cries, his verse, shrouded in pain,
Did he fall to Marduk? His holy blade unable to penetrate the well of soulless decay,
Or sentenced to death? His earthly vessel, castigated; for he could not obey,
Souls of the fallen Nephilim line the halls, my presence in this dying lair foretold--
Staff in hand, I cannot fail; for thy savior's blade, foretells the demons demise,
Alone at last, my heart turns cold.

VI

Infested Depths

Upon the day the untainted rise and across the rugged cavern, a righteous follower of the Lord will descend into the cavern at the base of the mount; the martyr will shed a lone tear inside the garden, and the cries of the sinners will flood paradise.

(The Epistle of Anacletus to the Priory 3.3)

From the demon infested depths, through their modern sacrifice,
From stolen knowledge, to the corrupted saintly verse,
The eye on the tomb stays true,
My mace, a beacon of hope illuminating the fallen,
Baptizing Belial's serpent demons in the way of Thy Father,
The blind prophets bow before the altar,
This pilgrimage to the garden foretold,
Control them? Repent? They must be christened in the way,
Enlighten the world; avenge Cain, with hallowed sway,
I must be strong; my faith cannot waver,
With every step, the revolting followers awaken in the eye,
My dark enemy is near.

For me, I have nothing to fear, nothing to hide,
Father, I am armed with your blessing, my survival prophesized,
Please, give me strength; help me turn the tide.

CANTO II

Lighting a Fire

VII

Be My Savior

Then I heard the majesty from heaven echo through the winds on earth and quake beneath the sea. Behold the mighty warrior and prepare for deliverance, for he is the way of The Father, and through his mortal vessel, tainted souls may be redeemed.
(The Epistle of Anacletus to the Priory 3.9)

Father, how much longer must I suffer through this ordeal?
How many more beasts must I slay? Or innocents saved?

Scarlet tears fall from lifeless eyes,
And the innocents beg for salvation,
Once an angelic warrior, now demonic prey,
Trapped in Levant, or oblivion, or worse,
Outside screams resonate upon splattered paths,
The keep is falling, and the lamps submit to the darkness,
Save you, save me, no one's safe here,
Nightmares, consume every breath,
Visions of dismay infest the living; fuel the undead,
Luscious flesh left sated by sin,
Help me; give me a sign! —I beg you, be my savior,
I have prayed to you, honored you,
Yet, you curse me with a path of loneliness,
How can I redeem the order, if I am destined to fail?

Father, how many evils exist in this poisoned land?
Will I have the strength to fulfill your confidence? To finally defeat evil?

VIII

Desolate Sands

From the depths came flashes of lightning, geysers of blood, and cries of unfathomable anguish; for the exiled beasts have risen before the throne and the undead walk. Seven fallen souls, seven evils to plague man- through the head and blood a lost light will shine, and the light will be known as redemption.
(The Epistle of Anacletus to the Priory 3.13)

In the distance, the moon comes to life,
Waking the souls of forgotten,
The succubus calls,
I cannot believe my eyes,
The dread,
The fear,
Her emotions consume the senses,
These demons are real, I know they are,
Hell hath overflowed into the depths of Levant,
Everywhere I look, I can hear them,
Their heavy breathing, their fervent moans,
In the sewers, in the tombs, and in my head,
Everywhere I turn, everything I see,
Helbah Oasis? A head?
Father, this cannot be real, this is not possible,
Yet, the sounds of wickedness plague me,
Tormenting everything that is; everything that was,
Damn you, infidel, what have you done?
These beasts, you have done this,
You have forsaken Levant in the name of Hell,
Unleashed the vileness of your unholy visage on humanity,
Desolate Sands, vials of blood?
These quests, my destiny, thousands of fiends line my wake,
Brimstone stains mark the walls,
The garish sighs of the elders grow louder,
Pulses quicken,

This could be my last breath,
Please, let me go...

In the distance, the sun stirs the echoes,
waking my pious soul,
reminding me of my journey-
and the pain I must face to save humanity.

IX

Lucifer Laughs

I ventured into the abyss, and there before me was a light, and inside light was hope,
and inside the hope was a mortal, and this mortal would be known
throughout the world as the one.
(The Epistle of Anacletus to the Priory 4.1)

From the angelic crater, an abominable darkness vanquished no more,
From the lure of power that could be, to the evil, and the souls of the pure,
Sin rises from the fissure, hope wavers-
The demons, the plagued, and the heretics ascend from the depths,
I must stand tall and honor Thy Father-
For only through his wisdom can Levant be reborn,
Azmodeus? Astaroth? Evil hordes of the impure,
Tormented souls or innocent prey-
This thankless quest, an immoral reminder of the dreadful shrouds of Hell,
The infernal ones rise again-
And Lucifer laughs at the despair.

For me, my crusade continues; my holy mace in hand-
Decomposed signs of destruction, bile and blood cover the sand,
For my destiny was foretold, I must sanctify this land.

X

Poisoned

Upon the fourth day, a great beast rose to challenge the almighty, and all of creation shuddered. From the winds of corruption and the tainted scepter, the unbearable darkness overwhelmed the gates, and faith disappeared within the tears of sorrow.
(The Epistle of Anacletus to the Priory 4.6)

Father, am I truly the chosen one? Am I worthy to defend your divinity?
How can I be worthy, I am but a mortal sinner and you are the Lord?

Look toward the gates, the most sacred angels await our entrance,
The Fountain of Forgiveness indeed lies inside dominion,
I sense this is a grave time for humanity,
Our evil prey have ascended into the Lords' domain,
Taking refuge within the divine haven,
The festering vermin, the fornicators, poisoning the golden sands with sin,
The signs of my mission lay before me,
This righteous path designed by God,
Time to go forth and continue my pilgrimage,
The scepter calls to me, tormenting me with the everlasting light,
Let us condemn these demons back to Hell,
And cleanse paradise in his name-
He is the one true Blessed Trinity and through his wisdom- is the way.

Father, I bow before thee, praying for a sign. Is redemption near?
Will you absolve me of my sins? Restore our order?

XI

Damnation

Then I saw an idol, and through this idol, I saw damnation.
Seven demons stand tall, six evils circling the throne, and the chasm of despair
growing deeper. Darkness rises from the South, and humanity pleads for mercy.
(The Epistle of Anacletus to the Priory 4.16)

Outside the monsoon rages,
Drowning the lamps with decaying tears of disease,
A perfect backdrop for the chaos raging along the hallowed halls,
On the tower, another innocent falls,
His remains consumed by putrefied rot,
I can see mysterious realities breed,
Their souls raped by the foul guardians of gluttony,
Their unforgotten sins sentencing them to serve in Hell,
I am too late to save these damned souls, yet many remain,
Sorrow engulfs my world, my faith falters,
I must destroy the evil; I must destroy Baal and cleanse this world.
My blade sharpens with the blood of every martyr,
Through this blood, truths become strengths, and enemies become dust.

XII

Join Me

Upon the desolate mount, within the ruins of Ekron, a crossroad shall appear,
and the darkness shall grip the forsaken. From this embrace, a forgotten warrior
shall rise from the depths, and through him, an army of the fallen shall perish,
and his name shall stand for eternity.
(The Epistle of Anacletus to the Priory 4.11)

Behold a new dawn,
The sun, rising like a blessed phoenix high above the mount,
I can see the brilliance of our labor at hand,
The prophecy of Our Lord, the Holy Father, lay before us.

Go forth and help me spread the gospel to the infidels,
Enlighten their feeble minds with our implements of sacred pain,
Soon, Levant shall be free, and the sun will rise,
All of our thoughts and prayers will unify.

Our brother Judas started preaching the word last night,
Converting the unwilling to our path,
Join him by increasing our army, as we destroy the hearts of sin,
As we cleanse the thoughtlessness from the delinquents.

Virgil appeared to me last night,
His message helped me visualize his odyssey into Satan's depths,
The legendary agony he encountered as the atrocities surrounded him,
Yet, his resolve remained steadfast through the wisdom of Thy Father.

Join me, and help me find Aamon and help destroy his vile idol.

CANTO III

Dunes of Despair

XIII

Protect Me

Behold, the marquise and the martyr, for their destiny grows from the tablet,
and their lives destined to be crossed within the sands of the inferno.
(Epistle of Anacletus to the Priory 5.1)

Father, for how long will these beasts rise from the depths?
How much longer must I survive? Or days will I be trapped in oblivion?

The sands erupt with the vengeance of Vesuvius,
And the infernal beasts decimate the pure,
For once, my passions led me toward the divine light,
Now, I stand facing the depths of anguish, or worse,
Everywhere I look, I see torment, hopelessness, and pain,
My faith, standing resolute with the glory of Thy Father,
And, culling the illicit deeds of the unholy trinity that surround me,
As the blood of the innocents, stain the golden grains before me,
I remain humbled by the power imbued into my soul,
When I was born, I was a sinner, now I stand revitalized by your conviction,
Help me; give me the strength! — Guide me through this wilderness,
Your blessing stills my panicked heart,
Yet, I wonder if my faith and blessed mace will be enough,
My destiny lay ahead, with your wisdom as my beacon,
Please Father; protect me!

Father, am I close to Baal, Moloch, or the scepter?
Am I truly righteous enough to succeed? Will Clement relent once I return?

XIV

Aamon Lives

When the Sun aligned with Jupiter, and Mars overwhelmed the Moon,
there was a fiery crack upon mount as the chthonic idol unleashed terror,
and the Earth quaked. From that quail and the seven souls,
a forsaken evil rose among men, and the forsaken hordes wept.
(The Epistle of Anacletus to the Priory 5.1)

Unspeakable truths appear before thee,
The idol, the vessel, the ancient evil wakes,
Consumed by lurid desires, her wickedness outweighs her blood,
How dare she sacrifice the maiden for her demonic needs?
And for what, the illicit allure of sin?
The emptiness, the pain, and the unjust torment-
Her despondent heart, a blackened soul pillaged by lies?
The Grand Marquise draws near, Aamon lives,
The path to redemption lies before me,
Am I strong enough? Do I have enough faith?
The splendor of Heaven calls—
--I am prepared to die.

XV

Penitence

On this day, Valor overwhelmed the righteous and he wept.
Through his despair, an unfathomable horde erupted with the force of
Vesuvius inside the sacred vestibule, and faith wavered.
(The Epistle of Anacletus to the Priory 5.5)

Indeed, Aamon stands before me, his minion readied for battle,
And, the horde of the unrepentant persist,
I must branch out and seize the heretic,
Cleanse their bodies of the impurities that flow within them,
My chalice cannot be poisoned by bitter wine from their veins,
Forgive them in the name of the holiest of holies,
And, convert them, for our mast sacred and everlasting creator is all.

These degenerates deserve naught their penitence,
They have forsaken his glory,
And, like Clement forsaken our Order,
I must make them understand that Thy Father is the way,
The most sacred angel in the universe,
With every blow, bless them with the divinity from the light,
And, purify their souls in the name of the Savior.

I must remain strong in the face of their deceit,
They will not fall willingly,
I must prey on their weakness; their guilt,
For their sins upon this land shall forever curse them to Hell,
The power of the Almighty will guide me,
Will transform these creatures to my divine path,
And, open their hearts for absolution.

I must be precise with my sermon,
The Sands of Jericho continue to fall freely.
And, the fruit of my pilgrimage awaits my blessing,

I can feel my pulse quicken with each step,
With every breath the demonic legion in front of me awaits my failure,
Baal, Moloch, and the scepter grow near,
The blood-soaked signs of redemption line the golden sands,
And, Aamon calls for reinforcements from the pit.

XVI

33 Beasts, 33 Souls

Upon the day when the ocean cries and the heavens fall, the tainted corridor
will open and a forbidden truth will rise. For through the divine beast, a hymn
will be sung, and tears of blood will guide the savior toward the keep.
(The Epistle of Anacletus to the Priory 5.9)

Father, how can this blight disregard the righteousness of our Lord?
Why must these sands of untruth plague the tainted meadow?

Precious Baphomet, the signs of disbelief are everywhere,
Why do the reverent dismiss the power of your scripture?
Do they not understand the true might of your presence?
The artifacts Helena discovered in your upon with the splintered cross;
Relics of divinity, revered for generations,
For in Eden, the serpent was slain, and man became man,
Through the golden dawn, eternity cursed forevermore,
Lush gardens transformed into desolate peaks,
Extinct virtues lost to the tree of knowledge, and the lies from the blasphemers,
33 beasts lined my path, 33 souls banished by my blades,
Still, the putrefying hordes of Levi infest my path,
How much longer to the throne, to the scourge of the innocents?
The scent of molding vestiges pulls me to the East, but my compass north,
Father, give me a sign,
The Sanguine Sea lay ahead and the depths of wrath overwhelm.

Father, why does the warmth of the mace flicker?
Is it not the divine marker that is destined to save our order?

XVII

Purgatory

And God spoke to the fervent, "Behold, the great deceiver stands before the altar,
waver naught; for he is legion incarnate, and his commands are wrought with sin.
" Go forth in the name of the lamb, and make the demon repent.
(The Epistle of Anacletus to the Priory 6.2)

The solitude masking the sands of the whirlpool lay before me;
Purgatories' maze stifles the air,
The vast tentacles grow across the horizon,
Smoldering carcasses of pillaged innocents but prey for Aamon,
Baal and his despondent hordes amass in Levant.

Father, give me the resolve to stand among men and face the despair,
The dead weep upon the dune sand the undead slumber in the bowels of Hades,
I can feel the warmth of the inferno,
The bile of the fallen kindles the flames,
Baal is near and Moloch with him.

He calls to me; waiting before his throne for my arrival,
Why? My presence would surely bring death and the light of the Lord,
But still, Father, something eludes me,
These demons, the devils do not quake with fear,
Their deeds, their wake, ridicule your wisdom.

My sins scorch my flesh;
And my eyes continue to well with dismay.

XVIII

Give Me a Sign

*A deafening howl was heard throughout Gods kingdom, as the infernal eclipse
faded into oblivion, and the Moon turned to blood. From the Heavens, darkness
descended onto the plain, and the souls of the damned cursed Levant once more.*
(The Epistle of Anacletus to the Priory 6.7)

Hugues, why? Do not let your faith waver,
I cannot give into the despair,
I must continue the battle,
Though, I can feel Aamon stalking my every move,
I will defeat him; all of them, I will purify Levant,
Father, show me the way,
...Help me find and destroy the beast!

Alas, the impaled disciples lead me to the throne,
Aamon stands before me.

Enlightened by wisdom,
The light again must sanctify this blessed ground,
Yet, as Aamon falls, the golden scepter eludes me,
Evil survives against the background of compassion,
A crimson flood now drowns the innocents,
The sounds of torture call from below,
...Help me find the resolve; lead me to Baal.

CANTO IV

One Last Hope

XIX

The Weeping Sun

Upon the land, Legion shall be reborn from the ashes, and all of humanity will suffer a great pestilence. From the wisdom of the pure, a spirit defiled by sin will rise; and the ultimate reaping will overtake Levant.
(The Epistle of Anacletus to the Priory 6.13)

Father, what have I done to deserve such torment?
Have I not done enough to be redeemed? Were our sins that heinous?

I stand before thee, humbled by your words,
Yet, the plagued souls of the fallen remain,
My faith is strong, still I pray for your strength to guide my blades,
How long until I break this shroud of evil;
To transcend this fractured dominion, and cleanse the souls of the intolerant,
In my heart, I can feel your warmth pulsate through my veins,
I am ready to face my true reality,
Aamon was resilient, his malicious deeds legendary,
Has he risen again, or has another escaped the depths of the Perditions lair?
The signs rise from every corner, every abyss.
Wickedness shrouds the light, and the Sun weeps,
The final battle draws near.

Father, why do the malefactors despise compassion?
Do the souls of the pure outweigh the soulless? Will we ever be safe?

XX

The Legion of Evil Wanes

As foretold at the beginning, the Nephilim fell, and the Sun, the Moon, and the Stars
blinked as they fell into obscurity; darkness smiled upon Levant and the day
shone naught for three phases, and sin overtook the garden.
(The Epistle of Anacletus to the Priory 7.3)

The warmth from the light calls to me,
The power from the slaughtered souls will guide me,
The foul stench of your minion will betray you,
I am closing the distance with every step,
And upon the altar, your reign of terror will end.

Your powers are already growing weak,
I can sense it, smell it,
Lotan was no match for my sanctified mace,
He seven heads wept, and begged for mercy, before I damned him back to Hell,
And soon, you will join him to face eternity.

You cannot win; your power is no match for the devout,
Hugues regained his faith, and your revolting brothers cried,
Now, through the rifts, the legion of evil wanes,
Can you hear the clock? Is Hell calling you home?
You cannot, will not survive.

Resheph has fallen; again, my mace cleansed the virulent sinners,
I can see you tremble, you are afraid,
Hugues was right, you have grown; yet, you still have much to learn,
You cannot defeat the Almighty,
You will never rule the world.

XXI

Thunder Reigns', Lightning Follows

And the abhorrent hordes were given the power over humanity by the fallen one,
and with their scythes, they drew blood, and with their eyes, they stole life;
and through the torment of man, the dark shroud of sin hardened.
(The Epistle of Anacletus to the Priory 7.7)

Something is clearly wrong, but what is it,
This smell is overwhelming, as the putrid pong of decay surrounds me,
The blood, the bile, the intestines; another evil has risen from the pit,
Carthage is under siege; I must set them free.

The golden rays of deceit, Hugues, Hells salvation must be near,
Evil signs overtake the soul,
Eternal conflict lines Satan's dreams, and legends cannot fear,
Silence still, moralities' enemies watch as sins take their toll.

There I stand, and see, Baal rise at night,
The fallen angel grows strong, and his reapers worse,
His blade of sorrow steals a life, my faith shudders at his might,
Questions I ponder deep, I must vanquish this curse.

Thunder reigns', lightning follows, as scarlet flows from flames of Molochs'
chambers,
I can see my salvation, and our redemption, inside the black depths of his eyes.

XXII

Emotions Churn

The redeemer spoke to the warrior, behold, evil shakes the foundations of the grand entrance as the innocents' tremble. Fear naught, for the savior will be sheltered from damnation, as the black horse turns pale and the tentacles of the pyre reach for the righteous
(The Epistle of Anacletus to the Priory 8.4)

Father, why must my pain grow with every step?
Will I have the fortitude to continue? Or have the strength to survive?

Inside my battered shell, the swirling whirlpool of desperation grows,
Covering my entrails with streaks of hopelessness,
The unrest escalating outside is inconceivable,
For Baal has conjured his minion, and my faith turns to fear,
Lost, my emotions churn…
… And the appendages long for my soul.

I can see unknown realities transcend belief,
Populating this disturbing world that has me enslaved,
A heart full of wisdom,
A mind full of questions,
Unfulfilled deeds yet to be done…
… And acts of depravity left in my wake,

Desolation fuels my sorrow,
Will I be strong enough to prevail?
Or, will these rancid downpours drown my light?
The veracities of despair ripen,
Baal's horde grows, infesting the fortress…
… And melancholy engulfs my world.
Father, how can you have faith in my actions, when I have naught faith in myself?
How can your consecrated armors last, as my blood shivers from fright?

XXIII

Ascension

And the visitor stood before the intolerant and professed,
"Behold, I am a vessel of faith and through my faithfulness, my mortal flesh
faced the temptation of sin and became one with the Lamb."
Fear naught in the depths of the lair; fidelity to the Lord will protect the righteous.
(The Epistle of Anacletus to the Priory 8.7)

Pillars of torment line the cavern,
The reminders of Baal are everywhere,
The carnage, the smoldering skin, and the infernal furnace ablaze with decadence,
What does this throng of ignorance see inside this labyrinth?
How could they curse their lineage to the bowels of Moloch?
Is it for the crops, forgiveness, or is it something that I cannot yet comprehend?
For them, I feel no pity, only disgust and hate,
Their salvation can only be found within the blood of the lamb,
Or possibly, from the contrition brought forth by my blades,
The symphony of their pain would be magnificent,
An angelic crescendo echoing throughout the corridors of Hell,
Fire and brimstone enlightening the blackest crevices and darkest days,
Behold the maggots as they fornicate before the effigy,
Is it nature's revenge, or just blindness to the Maker?
Even their canon proclaims the savior will be born unto a virgin,
And, like Lazarus rise from the dead,
All of the testaments, prophecy, covenants-their stone tablets blazing with law,
Nevertheless, they defile the Almighty, and disrespect the Word,
Can you hear their shrieks call to me?
The rancid smell of repugnant sin is unmistakable,
Baal is near; his malevolent bouquet floods the darkened sanctum,
The carcasses of the meek gasp for redemption within his lair,
Their remains spawning in the fiery moat of pus surrounding the tomb,
The churning tides of crimson sludge fueled by the wounds of the wretched,
I will not fail in my charge,
The purity of the devout will protect me,

SALVATION

As my pilgrimage is illuminated by the ash of the faithful,
For them, I need to succeed in my quest,
I must reclaim the scepter for the light,
And, finally, ascend to the right hand of the Father.

XXIV

Adrift in the Shadows

Within the tainted sanctum, one of the forsaken beasts gasped, and the herald
baptized the sinful followers in the venomous river flowing from the fallen ones veins.
The faithful bowed before the Lords' servant and professed, as it is foretold it is known,
for the Almighty is the Lamb, and the Lamb is thy God.
(The Epistle of Anacletus to the Priory 8.11)

Through darkened days and unknown specters
Mysteries shadow truths inside spiraling emotions-
Empty thoughts, and even stranger dreams, give way-
For my mind, realities fade; the scepter is within reach.

"Bow before me Baal, or the scars from my blade will be your absolution."

Stillness engulfs the vile depths, as silence penetrates the Nephilim,
Reverie smothers the calm- but still,
The forgotten rise and roam the abyss, protecting him,
Bodies fly, no escape, as their hunger is stronger than their will,
My blade overthrows the tyrants- solitude unbound
Calmness swallows thy heart: judgments unwound.

The gate, sacred seals, and demons rise-
And the dead walk with souls despised,
Foretold by scripture and desires once lost,
Mortal fears and open wounds survive the crossed-
Blessed implements stained by blood, opened doors,
For the path to deliverance rose upon unseen shores,
The chasm burns and the pure follow,
Forsaken by seraphim, adrift in the shallows.

"Moloch, rise before me and face the Lord's wrath, for through this blade,
your impurity can be forgiven."

43

SALVATION

Words are but verses that shall be composed,
Verses are but visions that must be transposed,
Revelations feed doubts; emptiness breeds fright
Choices wither- and reservations survive, at least for a night.

The truths- and the tainted flesh-cannot hide-
The souls of the damned drowned by pride,
Ancient riddles difficult to perceive,
An unfamiliar destiny left for me to conceive-
How this oracle grew-an opportunity for naught,
A mystery for sure, this scepter I have sought.

"Moloch, your tomb is near, release the scepter, and be baptized by light."

Through a vibrant flail and mighty shriek,
Moloch ascends from the inferno, to dine upon the meek,
Baal has fallen, disemboweled upon his throne,
My final trial lay ahead, redemption at hand.

CANTO IV

Wisdom Through Salvation

XXV

Seven Heads-Seven Diadems

Behold, the first archfiend fell to the divine blade, and the sands of oblivion turned to
blood. For beyond the idol, the secret covenant shattered and dark truths exposed.
(The Epistle of Anacletus to the Priory 9.1)

Father, why has this mantle obscured the light for so long?
My faith wavers in the face of this deception; will you guide me?

The legions of blasphemers surround the idol,
Nephilim blood-human eyes, lava, and bone; Moloch in the flesh,
The plague of deceit desecrates the bloodstained dunes of Levant,
Jacques, Hugues, why have you condemned me with your lies?
And the order, were we not worthy of the truth,
As you sit at the right hand of the beast,

How could we not see the reality that lay before us?
Seven heads-seven diadems, John the Revelator was right,
Rome is the--no, it cannot be real,
Canonic scripture, a gospel full of hollowness,
Here within this fouled realm, the spiteful face of the Maker at last revealed,
My virtues on high, I cannot-will not accept this fate,

Stand bastards, feel the deliverance alive in my blades,
The Scepter of Light lay upon the sludge,
Its righteousness drowned by the scales of sin in the hands of the wretched,
Jacques fell first, Hugues followed,
Their once blessed blood vanquished by the power of the light,
Their souls impaled upon the idol,

The relic calls to me, Moloch must not survive the night,
His bowels cleansed by the demonic crucifix he holds dear,
The staff must be mine; I must redeem the order, an undo the centuries of lies,
Like Judas, spread the true word of the Lord,

SALVATION

And expose the generations of usurpers and their septic history,
For the Lamb, is a Lamb, and the Almighty is the Baphomet.

Father, will you absolve me for my vicious acts?
Will you cleanse me of this affliction and have mercy on me?

XXVI

Vengeance

As the wind blows from the East, a tempest rages inside the inferno and Levant shudders.
Go forth with faith and rescue the scepter, for through the eternal light encased
in the sacred deity, the path to redemption will at last be illuminated.
(The Epistle of Anacletus to the Priory 9.6)

Look around,
Listen to the sinners disperse,
Their fetid pulse betrays them,
Silent prayers echo through the emptiness,
I can sense Moloch guiding them,
Their insipid scents draw me closer to the black veil,
Can you feel it inside?
Father, can you hear the banquet of sin call to me?
I know you do,
I bow before you pledging my faith for your wisdom,
Our order must partake in this communion.

Blessed be, oh, mighty Baphomet,
Thank you for enlightening my journey with your divinity,
Opening your mouth to reveal the true path of righteousness,
Did you leave the malefactors for us and out order?
Or did you devour them for desecrating your sanctity?
I pray to thee for guidance,
Protect me as I pass through these caverns of misery,
The search for the scepter leads me through this labyrinth,
My journey to Mount Heres nears an end,
Only there, may the true providence be revealed,
Only there, will heaven be rebuilt.

Look around,
Listen to the silence
Through the horizon, I can sense another amongst the Moloch's' traitors,

SALVATION

Can you feel him too?

His pheromones betray him

His blackened heart calls to me for salvation,

Yet, the cravings flowing through his veins are strong,

It is he, whose baptism upon the embers of darkness has been foretold?

Like Baal, he will feel the vengeance of my blade,

And, I will reclaim the scepter for the Lord,

At last, our redemption will be at hand.

XXVII

I Bow and Pray

*Across the canyon, a fire scars the mount and an infernal temple ascends
from the ashes. A lone warrior set forth from the garden with faith, and the
followers sunk in prayer, for Armageddon was at hand.*
(The Epistle of Anacletus to the Priory 9.9)

Within the depths of Levant, a final path of pilgrimage appears on the cliff,
The relic, the fiends, a mass of repugnant creatures, for as far as one can see;
The dismembered and disemboweled walk, their spiteful blades concealed,
Forlorn, and alone, life's emptiness at hand, please help me.

From Nephalem blood, and sated tears,
From the tainted thorns, and seven souls, the immoral unleashed the darkness,
Help, Father, hear my call, please sate my fears,
Entrails fall, scarlet flows, and still, revolting legions swell.

At last, I stand before the thrown, my mighty mace in hand,
In the abyss where the kingdom reigns, decaying maggot's plea,
My body is torn, and every test I have passed,
And as the moon fades across the land, my faith resolute, I bow and pray.

XXVIII

Redemption at Last

*Then I saw a mighty warrior rise from the pandemic, embraced by the Almighty, and
ordained by the Lord; his appearance prophesized in scripture, his valor legendary, and
through his sacrifice, he would become known throughout the kingdom as Salvation.*
(The Epistle of Anacletus to the Priory 9.9)

Suddenly the message is clear; my destiny at hand,
Embers to ashes, day to night,
The divine tapestry falls silently into the ravine,
And the spirits of the lost engulf this realm,
Joining me in this final battle for salvation,
Ignite the torch, open the void, and raise the dead,
For Moloch and Elyon will not bow before me.

This night if foreign, the seraphs have vanished,
They cower before the altar as the horde readies for battle,
My minion does not quiver, as I ready my mace for deliverance,
The holy vestige burns with the power of million lumens,
The sins of the masses fueling the inferno,
And silence befalls the guilty,
Their baptism closes, as my hand grasps the holy conduit of salvation.

My blade slices Elyon,
His venomous abdomen erupts like Etna,
A river of blood and bile drown the sinners in limbo,
Their bodies line the chasm as the statues line Saint Peters,
Moloch must be next; his horns, the heart of a whore, he must fall,
My pulse quickens as the look of fear overwhelms this fouled sanctuary,
The flavor untouched, thrill unmatched-the scepter draws near.

Moloch stands before me, the flames of Heaven consuming his blackened soul,
The revolting stench masks the depths of sin,
With centuries of viral rot infesting his every move,

My staff enters his disgusting void, blood oozing from the festering bosom,
Panic rises from the calm as thunder reigns down from the profane charlatan,
The heretical lies masked within the sacred trinity revealed,
And the true face of divinity will finally see the light of day.

Charcoal to embers, night to day,
The Scepter of Light is one with the Almighty,
And the redemption of our order may finally be at hand,
The demonic hordes of the unfaithful bow before thee,
The fallen star has returned, I can feel it,
My passageway lay ahead, as the moon rises about the sanguine fields of despair,
Mount Heres has been cleansed; my work here is complete.

XXIX

The Fallen Star Nears

As the vile beasts lay before the altar, the mighty warrior bowed before the Father and professed his sins. From the North a flash of light appeared in the sky and Heres shuddered, for the Redeemer has been forgiven, and his passage from Levant was granted.
(The Epistle of Anacletus to the Priory 10.2)

Father, tonight, all my prayers will be answered,

Baal, Moloch, and Elyon lay impaled upon the altar,

Forbidden replies rise from the depths, and the fallen star nears,

All of my atrocities will at last be justified by the remnants of the Templars,

As night descends, the darkness laughs in the shadows,

The rogue minion of sinners surround me; yet, I am alone,

A torrential rage echoes from beyond the mount,

Alive, the scepters light guides me,

My heart races, and hope builds within my mind,

I can see the Jordan, water to wine,

My secret elixir and life,

Still, my true destiny lay ahead upon my return,

I watch the venom swirl in the well,

I see deliverance, a lone tear,

Scars of redemption glisten in moonlight,

My fetid wounds of truth, and wounds of redemption,

The secrets you hold are no longer a mystery,

The transfusion nears an end; I must reveal the truth about the deceiver,

The bloodline must be revealed to the congregation,

Placenta filled vats await their call within the basilica,

The sanguine river to again flow and the most holy trinity illuminate the urn,

Ragged flesh breathes, their baptism at hand,

Answer my cry to thee, Father,

My quest at last complete, as the Scepter of Light will burn bright,

And through this light, forever will be,

Silence screams inside the chamber,

And liberation will at last for perpetuity,

My prayers; my gospel echoing through eternity,

This night, breathe life into my soul,

And allow my journey to be known to all humanity,

For my epitaph complete, and I stand humbled before thee,

Make Clement proud and renounce Phillip and the lies,

From the void, and through the word of the Lamb,

Bless those of lives lost and love anew,

My mortal heart beats again upon this knoll and Levant fades into oblivion,

And at last, the sins of the world can be forgiven.

XXX

Salvation

Upon the day when the horsemen rose in the shadow of the cathedral and the tainted bloodline was at last disclosed, the martyr stood before the blade and professed the true wisdom of the Lamb. And through the chains the mighty warrior wept, for the blasphemers and heretics betrayed the blessed word of the Lord.
(The Epistle of Anacletus to the Priory 10.8)

Such a dark day in the world,
Phillip and the heretics have again defiled the Order-the true Messiah,
And you, Father, are left to weep among the damned,
The four horses are drawn, our finality at hand,
Not by the masses that pray,
But, from the hypocrisy of medieval royalty that prey,
On our flesh and your sacred secrets?
Should not it be they, who suffer for following the false prophet,
The sinner who hid behind his disciples,
And worse, the women and children of Judea,
Spouting lies of redemption and tormenting the righteous,
Preaching abstinence instead of indulgence,
And in turn, creating turmoil in the perfect world.

.. ..

Through it all, you stood tall in the face of the blasphemers,
The destroyers of forged faith who were blind,
Failing to harness the power of your minions,
By creating a day of homage of their transgressions, they granted you eternal life,
History crying tears of truths in your name,
Even now, after trespassing into our sanctum and pilfering the scepter,
You will never be forgotten, as they will never eclipse your light that burns inside the relic,
You Baphomet, will live forever, as will our Order,
Like me, and my brothers, your followers will bleed for you,

Carrying on the traditions passed down by the strong,

Your enigma, a mystery to most, but a reality for the devoted,

Father, forgive these sinners for they know not the depths of their actions,

For through your wisdom and sacrifice, Salvation is upon us.

ABOUT THE AUTHOR

Born and raised in the shadows of Appalachia, Mark A. Mihalko is cunningly creative with a flair for the freakish. An experienced fiction and nonfiction writer, Mark is the author of three books, *After the Static*, *Searching the Abyss*, and *Walking Before Dawn*, and has seen his works published in multiple online and print media outlets such as *Mysteries*, *FATE*, *Horrotica*, *Haunted Times*, *Doorways* and *Revenant Magazine*. He was also lucky enough to be the focus of the Poet of the Hours for the *Graveyard Press*, the official webzine of the Vampire Nation.

Mark holds a Bachelor of Fine Arts in Creative Writing for Entertainment from Full Sail University. While he has a long way to go to achieve his goal of writing a multimedia/ multi-platform horror themed universe, he is constantly searching for new projects and outlets to share his twisted interpretations of reality.

Made in the USA
Columbia, SC
27 September 2017